LEON

Smoothies, Juices & Cocktails

NATURALLY FAST RECIPES

LEON

NATURALLY FAST RECIPES

Smoothies, Juices & Cocktails

By Henry Dimbleby, Kay Plunkett-Hogge, Claire Ptak & John Vincent

PHOTOGRAPHY BY GEORGIA GLYNN SMITH · DESIGN BY ANITA MANGAN

conran
OCTOPUS

Contents

Introduction

'Cheers'. 'Skol'. 'Your good health'. There is a reason why we have different sayings for drinking. They mark an occasion. A morning ritual. A birthday. A rite of passage.

In this book, we have assembled the full family of liquid refreshment. The world convention of drinks. Each with their own pin-on name card and information pack. From (sparkly) sandal-wearing smoothies to the sassiest of cocktails.

You will find the Leon Power Smoothie. (It won't help you rule the world. It's much better than that). You'll also find coolers for the summer, warmers for the winter, and a punch, not for the first day of the month, but for Hallowe'en.

We are grateful to the work of wider Leon friends (from the wider Leon family). They include 'Uncle' Ian who, for a while managed our restaurants, and who's a charming and talented man. And to Tom Ward who is opening his own pork store. And Vince Jung who owns the Formosa Café in Hollywood (that is in America, America) who has allowed us to put his Margarita in lights, and really big letters.

A manager of a football club said that each time he wrote his team sheet he would get excited. That's how we feel about this collection of drinks. If we had them in the dressing room before kick off we'd say: 'We've been through a lot. We have trained hard. We've been up together at daybreak. We have been there for each other on our first dates. We are tasty as individuals. But we are most powerful as a team. So go out there and give everyone who has bought this book what they deserve. A drink for the darkest of early starts. A drink for the hottest of days. For the bitterest of snowfalls. For when they announce their engagement. For when they want to forgive or forget. Go out there and create magic.'

We hope you feel the same.

Basic Tools

Microplane zester

For getting the zest off citrus fruits. If you are using a traditional zester you will need to chop it finely. Make sure you aren't so seduced by the microplane's easy action that you absentmindedly shred the white pith – it is very bitter.

Measuring spoons

Have one set and use them for everything. Whether this is superstition or not, we find that different sets seem to vary slightly.

Measuring jug

Always WEIGH water on the scales. You can use a measuring jug to get the rough quantity, but for many recipes the jug is not accurate enough.

Speed peeler

Owning any other kind of peeler is a form of madness – a bit like when Björn Borg tried to make his comeback in professional tennis using a wooden racket. The speed peelers are by far the most effective.

Paring knife

For all those little jobs: e.g. freeing cakes from tins, trimming fruits, or scoring bread dough.

Juicer (or reamer)

Great for getting all the juice out of a small amount of fruit. Cheap, easy to clean, efficient, durable, beautiful, simple and safe.

Stick blender

For making fruit purées, seed milks, bringing chocolate and butter mixes back if they have split, and mixing flavours.

Ice cream machine

A complete luxury, as you can make great ice cream without one. On the other hand, you could have a lot of fun with it and it saves time.

Bird's beak

A specialist knife for trimming fruit into particularly pleasing shapes.

Zester

For when you need a hit of zesty flavour and you are going to strain out the zest, for example in a poaching liquid or ice cream base. You can also make delicate strands of candied zest by poaching them in a simple syrup.

SMOOTHIES & JUICES

Energy Booster Smoothie

SERVES 4 · PREPARATION TIME: 5 MINUTES · COOKING TIME: NONE · ♥ WF GF DF V

The guv'nor of all smoothies. This bad boy (sorry, good boy – very good boy) is packed full of healthy omega-3 and is stuffed with all the vitamins in the alphabet. The secret weapon is avocado – one of nature's finest superfoods. As well as adding essential amino acids, it also brings a gorgeous creaminess to the smoothie.

1 **avocado**
2 handfuls EACH of any three of the following:
  hulled strawberries, **raspberries, blueberries,**
  blackberries, bilberries, logan berries
200ml **orange juice**
1 tablespoon **linseed**, plain or toasted
2 ripe **bananas**

1. Pop everything into the blender – it's not an exact science, just bung 'em all in – and whizz until smooth.

TIPS

* When berries are in season, use them fresh – then freeze a load to use through the winter. Just pop them straight into the blender, frozen, for a delicious chilled smoothie.

* Add soya milk instead of the orange juice if you like. If you do, add a splash of honey or agave nectar to replace the sweetness the orange juice provides.

Strawberry Power Smoothie

SERVES 2 • PREPARATION TIME: 5 MINUTES • COOKING TIME: NONE • ✓ WF GF V

When we introduced this to our menu, one of our regulars described it as 'another small step for mankind'.

1 small **banana**
a small handful of **fresh** or
   frozen strawberries
60g **oats**
1 tablespoon **clear honey**
125ml **Greek yoghurt**
150ml **whole milk**

TIPS

* If you can't get your hands on fresh or frozen strawberries, you can add strawberry jam.

1. Peel the banana, and hull the strawberries.

2. Put all the ingredients into a blender and blitz together.

Blackberry Power Smoothie

SERVES 2 • PREPARATION TIME: 5 MINUTES • COOKING TIME: NONE • ✓ WF GF V

We bring this on to the menu in autumn, when it's getting a little parky for strawberries.

1 small **banana**
a small handful of **fresh** or
   frozen blackberries
60g **oats**
1 tablespoon **clear honey**
125ml **Greek yoghurt**
150ml **whole milk**

TIPS

* If you can't get your hands on fresh or frozen blackberries, you can add blackberry jam.

1. Peel the banana, and pick over the blackberries.

2. Put all the ingredients into a smoothie machine or a food processor and blitz them together.

OPPOSITE FROM TOP: CARROT, ORANGE & GINGER JUICE; STRAWBERRY POWER SMOOTHIE; GABRIELA'S GREEN SMOOTHIE; KIWI BREAKFAST SMOOTHIE; HATTIE'S SUPER-HEALTHY ALMOND SMOOTHIE; BLACKBERRY POWER SMOOTHIE.

Kiwi Breakfast Smoothie

SERVES 4 • PREPARATION TIME: 5 MINUTES • COOKING TIME: NONE • ♥ ✓ WF GF V

For those who don't fancy bananas, this smoothie makes a great substitute.

> 2 **kiwi fruits**
> a large handful of **berries** of your choice
> 1 teaspoon **linseeds**
> 1 teaspoon **sunflower seeds**
> 125ml **Greek yoghurt**
> 125ml **fresh orange juice**

1. Peel the kiwis and wash the berries.

2. Put all the ingredients into a smoothie machine or a blender and blitz together until smooth.

Carrot, Orange & Ginger Juice

SERVES 2 • PREPARATION TIME: 5 MINUTES • COOKING TIME: NONE • ♥ ✓ WF GF DF V

A great cold-buster, this has become a regular on the Leon menu.

> 3 **carrots**
> a thumb-sized piece of **fresh ginger**
> 500ml **freshly squeezed orange juice**

1. Peel the carrots and the ginger.

2. Juice both in a juicing machine and pour into a large jug.

3. Add the freshly squeezed orange juice and mix well.

TIPS

* If you only have a carton of orange juice, this is a great way to pep it up.

Gabriela's Green Smoothie

SERVES 6 • PREPARATION TIME: 5 MINUTES • COOKING TIME: NONE • ♥ ✓ WF GF V

Gabriela is a friend of ours who specializes in raw food. This is not one for the faint-hearted. Some of us love it, for others it is inedible. It is made possible by the fact that raw kale is surprisingly sweet – try biting off a piece.

4 **kale leaves**, stalks removed
250ml **milk** or a dairy-free alternative,
   e.g. **rice milk**, **soya milk** or **nut milk**
1 **banana**
1 **pear**
1 tablespoon **honey**
1 tablespoon **almond butter**
1 tablespoon **cocoa powder**
   (or cacao powder)

TIPS

* If you can't find almond butter, use peanut butter.

1. Start by blending the kale with the milk and 150ml of water until there are no more chunks or bits.

2. Add the rest of the ingredients and blend well.

Hattie's Super-Healthy Almond Smoothie

SERVES 2 • PREPARATION TIME: 5 MINUTES • COOKING TIME: NONE • ♥ WF DF GF V

And for those who are looking for something dairy free . . .

1 **kiwi fruit**
1 **banana**
2 large handfuls of **berries** –
   whatever is in season
8 **almonds**, skins on

2 heaped tablespoons **oats**
1 tablespoon **pumpkin seeds**
1 tablespoon **sunflower seeds**
250ml **rice milk**, **almond milk**
   or **soya milk**

1. Peel the kiwis and the banana. Wash the berries.

2. Put all the ingredients into a smoothie machine or a blender and blitz together until smooth.

Cucumber Cooler

MAKES 2 LITRES (BEFORE ICE) • ♥ ✓ WF GF DF V

This might just be the most beautiful-looking drink in the world, and it's refreshing too.

1 **cucumber**
1 **lime**
1.5 litres **cold water**

1. Peel the cucumber, discarding the peel. Then, still using the peeler, keep peeling the flesh into long ribbons, turning it as you go. Drop the cucumber ribbons straight into your favourite jug, and keep making more until you get to the seeds.

2. Squeeze in the juice of the lime, and add the water and lots of ice.

Melon Fizz

MAKES 1.4 LITRES • ♥ ✓ WF GF DF V

1 ripe **cantaloupe melon**
juice of 2 **limes**
1 litre cold **fizzy water**

1. Peel the melon and remove the seeds. Chop the flesh and blend it in a food processor with the juice of 1 lime.

2. Pour through a sieve or fine strainer, into a wide-necked jug or bowl, squeezing as much of the juice through as you can.

3. Top up with fizzy water and serve.

OPPOSITE FROM LEFT: SPARKLING STRAWBERRY COOLER; CUCUMBER COOLER; MELON FIZZ.

18

Toph's Strawberryade

SERVES 2 • PREPARATION TIME: 5 MINUTES• COOKING TIME: NONE • WF GF V

180ml **water or sparkling water**
1–2 tablespoons **agave nectar**
   (depending how sweet you like it –
   I like it tart, so I just use 1 tablespoon)
50ml **lemon juice** (about 2 lemons)
5–6 **strawberries**, hulled and chopped

1. Blend all of the above together (add a little ice if you wish, but if you do, then drop the water).

Sparkling Strawberry Cooler

MAKES: I.4 LITRES • PREPARATION TIME: 2 MINUTES• COOKING TIME: NONE • ♥ ✓ WF GF DF V

300g **strawberries**
6 **mint leaves**
juice of 1 **lemon**
2 tablespoons **honey**
1 litre cold **sparkling water**

1. Whizz everything except the water in a blender.

2. Add ice to the blender if you wish.

3. Transfer to a jug and mix in the sparkling water, and serve.

Watermelon Slurpie

SERVES 2–4 • PREPARATION TIME: 10 MINUTES • COOKING TIME: NONE • ♥ WF GF V

All over Thailand, you see carts advertising *ponlamai puun* or 'spun fruit'. These icy cool fruit drinks come in myriad flavours – perfect for the tropical heat. Our favourite is the watermelon – pink, refreshing and sweet.

> 1 smallish ripe **watermelon** (2–3kg), peeled,
> deseeded and diced, preferably chilled
> ½ teaspoon **salt**
> a few **ice cubes**
> 2 tablespoons **Simple Syrup** (see page 32)

1. Whiz up the watermelon in a blender with the salt and ice cubes. Only add the simple syrup if the watermelon is not sweet enough.

TIPS

* To be very Thai you could finish the slurpie off with a spoonful or two of sweetened condensed milk or some coconut milk.
* Add a few fresh mint leaves and a squeeze of lime.

Date Shake

SERVES 2–4 • PREPARATION TIME: 5 MINUTES • COOKING TIME: NONE • WF GF V

> 15 **whole dates**, pitted and roughly chopped
> 250ml **unsweetened soya milk**
> 1 ripe **banana**, peeled and chopped
> 2–4 **ice cubes**
> a pinch of **ground cinnamon** or **ground cardamom**

1. Put everything into a blender and whizz on high power until it's really well blended: thick and creamy. Pour and serve immediately.

TIPS

* You could use whole milk or skimmed milk or rice milk – it's up to you.
* Try replacing the banana with a scoop of good vanilla ice cream or another handful of pitted dates.

COCKTAILS

Soul Fruit Cup

SERVES 6 • PREPARATION TIME: I MINUTE • COOKING TIME: NONE • WF GF V

Our friend Giles runs his own company called Soul Shakers, travelling the world making cocktails at some of the best parties in the world (lucky boy). He put together a cocktail bar at Henley for the Regatta and served this drink as his version of Pimm's. Perfect to sip on a hot summer's day, while others work up a sweat.

100ml **gin**
75ml **Campari**
100ml **sweet vermouth**
150ml **pink grapefruit juice**
juice of 2 **lemons**
6–8 slices of **cucumber**
lemonade (homemade or bottled)
strawberries and **mint**, to garnish (optional)

1. Pour the alcohol, grapefruit juice and lemon juice into a jug.

2. Add the cucumber and lemonade and stir.

3. Pour into iced glasses and garnish with strawberries and/or mint if you like.

Leon Summer Punch

SERVES 6 • PREPARATION TIME: 5 MINUTES • COOKING TIME: NONE • WF GF V

Think summer, all your best friends, your back garden, a balmy evening and an England World Cup victory.

16 **strawberries**
2 **pears** (nice and ripe)
150ml **Simple Syrup** (see page 32)
150ml **vodka**
120ml **lemon juice**
bottle of **prosecco**

1. Blend the strawberries and pears to make a simple purée, adding the simple syrup to sweeten.

2. Put the purée into a jug and mix in the vodka and lemon juice.

3. Top with prosecco and stir. Pour into champagne flutes and toast the Queen.

The Rude Boi

SERVES 1 • PREPARATION TIME: 2 MINUTES • COOKING TIME: NONE • WF GF V

Here's a tropical-inspired non-alcoholic cocktail for the kids, which we invented for Kay's nephews Alex and Alastair when they were younger. The high point in its genesis was the time Alastair discovered the cocktail shaker, and that fizzy drinks don't respond well to shaking, all in the same afternoon.

ice
shop-bought **mango and passion fruit smoothie**
ginger beer

TIPS

* You can substitute the ginger beer for sparkling pineapple and grapefruit drink if you prefer.

1. Fill a Collins glass with ice. Pour in 1 measure of the mango and passion fruit smoothie. Top up with ginger beer. Stir to blend and serve at once.

The Spritz

SERVES 2 • PREPARATION TIME: 2 MINUTES • COOKING TIME: NONE • WF GF V

The Venetian drink of choice. It's cool, bittersweet and colourful – just what you need for a party.

a dash of **Aperol** or **Campari** per glass
250–300ml **prosecco** (or **white wine and sparkling water**)
a small bowl of **ice**

2 chunks of **orange** (preferably sanguinella or blood orange)
2 **green olives** in brine, rinsed

1. Pour a dash of Aperol or Campari into each glass.

2. Top up to about half full with the prosecco or white wine and sparkling water. Pop a cube of ice in.

3. Skewer an orange chunk and an olive on each of 2 long cocktail sticks and place one in each glass. Serve with the bowl of ice on the side.

FROM LEFT: THE RUDE BOI; THE SPRITZ; VINCE JUNG'S MARGARITA.

Vince Jung's Margarita

SERVES 1 • PREPARATION TIME: 2 MINUTES • COOKING TIME: NONE • WF GF V

Kay's friend Vince is the third-generation owner of the landmark Hollywood bar, the Formosa Café, which has been serving everyone from movie stars to hoodlums since... well... it depends on who you talk to, but no one's really sure. Vince's margaritas are the business.

> 60ml **silver tequila**
> 30ml **Cointreau**
> the juice from 1½ **limes**
> 45ml **Simple Syrup** (see below)

1. Fill a metal cocktail shaker with ice and add all the ingredients. Shake briskly. Serve on the rocks or straight up in a salt-rimmed glass, and garnish with a wedge of lime.

Simple Syrup

A cocktail staple, this is super-easy to make and will see you through countless margaritas and other cocktails.

> 200g **caster sugar**
> 200ml **water**

1. Over a low to medium heat, mix the sugar and water together in a pan until the sugar is completely dissolved. Don't allow to boil.

2. Once it's all dissolved, set the pan aside to cool, then decant the syrup into a jam jar or bottle with a good fitting lid and store until you need it.

TIPS

* Be sure to sterilize your jam jar or bottle first.

* Simple syrup is also now available to buy in bottles at most supermarkets.

Kamomilla Fizz

SERVES I • PREPARATION TIME: 5 MINUTES • COOKING TIME: NONE • WF GF V

This is a slightly more taxing drink, for those of you who fancy yourselves as cocktail connoisseurs. It was invented for the International Finlandia Vodka Cup in 2006 and won the best long drink award. We served bucketloads at the Big Chill the same year. The camomile and cucumber work beautifully together, and it's a great long summer drink. You can substitute the vodka with gin, which also works really well (it's known as a 10cc).

> 3 slices of **cucumber** (about the thickness of a pound coin)
> ½ a **lemon**, cut into 4 wedges
> 25ml **Camomile Tea Syrup** (see below)
> 40ml **vodka**
> **ice**
> **sparkling water** or **soda water**

1. In a cocktail shaker, muddle the cucumber and 3 of the lemon wedges with the camomile tea syrup. Muddle it quite hard to work the juice and oil out of the lemon.

2. Add the vodka and ice and shake for a good 10 seconds. Strain into an ice-filled highball glass.

3. Top with sparkling water or soda. Garnish with the remaining lemon wedge. Kippis!

Camomile Tea Syrup

Make a strong brew of camomile tea – about 3 teabags in 200ml of hot water. Leave it to stand for 5 minutes. Remove the teabags and add 200g of caster sugar, then stir until the sugar has dissolved and leave to cool.

BEHIND THE SCENES at a Leon party...

Champagne Cocktail

SERVES 1 • PREPARATION TIME: 2 MINUTES • COOKING TIME: NONE • ♥ ✓ WF GF DF V

The perfect way to toast the New Year – in Scotland or elsewhere.

Angostura bitters
1 **sugar cube**
brandy
Champagne

1. Shake a couple of drops of Angostura on to the sugar cube and pop it into the bottom of a Champagne glass.

2. Pour on a little brandy. It is meant to be just a dash, but they say that fortune favours the bold.

3. Top up the glass with Champagne.

TIPS

*   You can use cava or prosecco or any dry sparkling white wine instead of Champagne (we normally do).

*   If you don't like brandy, you can leave it out. The original recipe doesn't include it.

SUMMER COOLERS

Fabulous Iced Lollies

PREPARATION TIME: 10 MINUTES • FREEZING TIME: OVERNIGHT (MINIMUM 2½ HOURS) • ♥ ✓ WF DF GF

Three grown-up iced lollies to cool you down on a hot summer's day. Each recipe makes lollies for 6 – you just need to pick which flavour to make first.

Strawberry Lolly

♥ ✓ WF DF GF V

600g **strawberries**, hulled
3 level teaspoons **fructose**
1 tablespoon **vodka**

Mango Lolly

♥ ✓ WF DF GF V

2kg **mango flesh**
3 level teaspoons **fructose**
1 tablespoon **vodka**

Baileys Lolly

✓ WF GF V

500ml **double cream**
3 level teaspoons **fructose**
3 tablespoons **Baileys**

1. Put all the ingredients into a blender and blend until smooth.

2. Divide equally between lolly moulds and push in the sticks (or cut-off straws).

3. Put in the freezer until firm.

TIPS

* The vodka brings out the flavour of the fruit. Leave the alcohol out if you want to avoid sedating your children.

* Create a rocket ship (see opposite) – this is tricky but rewarding. Freeze each of these ices in individual layers one after the other. Then drizzle a little melted chocolate on top (make sure the lolly is really cold first), and sprinkle on some space dust or sherbet. Cool on a sheet of greaseproof paper in the freezer.

Champagne Granita

SERVES 4–6 • PREPARATION TIME: 10 MINUTES • FREEZING TIME: 3-4 HOURS • ♥ WF GF DF V

A lovely light way to end a meal. Or, if you are feeling extravagant, to serve as a palate cleanser between the starter and the main course.

100g **caster sugar**
200ml **water**
325ml **Champagne** (½ a bottle)
juice of 1 **lemon**

1. Dissolve the sugar and water together in a pan over a moderate heat. Stir in the Champagne. Add lemon juice to taste.

2. Freeze in a roasting tray or other container that is shallow and wide, but will fit into your freezer. Every 30 minutes, use a whisk to stir and break up the ice that has formed, until all the liquid has turned into paper-thin ice shards.

We originally wanted to do an absinthe granita, one that would make a party swing. Sadly the stuff was so alcoholic that we couldn't get it to freeze, leaving us with a lethal, ice-cold absinthe syrup. Best to stick to Champagne really.

CLAIRE

TIPS

* You can play around with granitas as much as you want. Sharp rosé wine and fruit work well together, as do coffee, and vodka.

* Different alcohols also go well with different fruits. The alcohol can really bring out the flavour of a fruit, lifting it and making it more complex. Try Grand Marnier with orange, kirsch with cherries or pineapple. There are some wonderful small distilleries cropping up that are mixing fruits and alcohol. You can find pear, greengage, quince and others. They are worth seeking out.

OPPOSITE TOP: CHAMPAGNE GRANITA, LEFT: QUINCE GRANITA, RIGHT: CLEMENTINE GRANITA.

Clementine Granita

SERVES 4–6 • PREPARATION TIME: 5 MINUTES • COOKING TIME: 10 MINUTES • ♥ WF GF DF V

A light, fruity granita for winter refreshment.

100ml **water**
50g **caster sugar**
300ml **clementine juice**, strained

1. Combine the water and sugar over a low heat to make a syrup. Cool completely.

2. Stir in the strained clementine juice.

3. Freeze in a roasting tray or other container that is shallow and wide, but will fit into your freezer. Every 30 minutes, use a whisk to stir and break up the ice that has formed, until all the liquid has turned into paper-thin ice shards.

TIPS

* Serve with grapefruit or orange sections, in pretty glass cups.

* It is also nice with a crisp buttery biscuit.

Quince Granita

SERVES 4–6 • PREPARATION TIME: 25 MINUTES • COOKING TIME: 2 HOURS
FREEZING TIME: 5 HOURS • ♥ WF GF DF V

A more scented, full-bodied granita, and a lovely way to finish off an autumn dinner.

1½ **quinces**
300g **caster sugar**
700ml **water**
1 **vanilla pod**, split in half lengthwise
juice of ½ a **lemon**

1. Peel and quarter the quinces. Put the sugar, water and vanilla pod into a saucepan and stir to dissolve the sugar. Bring to the boil.

2. Add the quinces and the lemon juice. Simmer for 1–2 hours, or until the quinces are tender when pierced and rosy in colour.

3. Remove the quinces from the syrup and core them. Remove the vanilla pod.

4. Purée the quinces and syrup together, then add some water to adjust the consistency so it's less thick.

5. Freeze in a roasting tray or other container that is shallow and wide, but will fit into your freezer. Every 30 minutes, use a whisk to stir and break up the ice that has formed, until all the liquid has turned into paper-thin ice shards.

TIPS

* Quinces are thick and fluffy when puréed and lend themselves very well to being frozen. Be sure to cook them long enough so that they are tender.

* Add a teaspoon or two of honey to the purée as a variation. Honey and quince have an affinity for each other.

Apple Sorbet

SERVES 4–6 • PREPARATION TIME: 25 MINUTES • FREEZING TIME: UP TO 5 HOURS • ♥ WF GF DF V

We call this apple sorbet, but apple snow might be a better description. It is light and fluffy and pure as the driven ... The egg white and gelatine add protein, which gives the sorbet its gorgeous texture.

500ml **cloudy apple juice**
50g **caster sugar**
1 teaspoon **powdered gelatine**
1 **free-range egg white**
a splash of **apple brandy** (optional)

1. Gently heat 250ml of the apple juice with the sugar in a small saucepan.

2. In another pan, soften the gelatine with the remaining apple juice off the heat and then heat it gently to dissolve. Once dissolved, combine the two liquids and pour into a container to cool. When cooled, place in the fridge until ready to freeze.

3. Whisk the egg white to soft peaks and fold it into the chilled sorbet base. Add the apple brandy, if using, then pour into an ice cream machine and freeze according to the manufacturer's instructions.

TIPS

* Use a high-quality tart apple juice, or, even better, juice your own.

* Try substituting pear, peach, watermelon or grape juice for the apple. If they are very sweet you might need a squeeze of lemon to add some acidity.

Blood Orange & White Wine Jelly

SERVES 6 • PREPARATION TIME: 10 MINUTES
COOKING TIME: 10 MINUTES • ♥ WF GF DF (V IF YOU USE VEGETARIAN GELATINE)

There is something about the limpid tremble of a lightly set jelly that is devilishly alluring. This one is based on a recipe from Richard Olney's 1970 classic *The French Menu Cookbook*. His recipe includes instructions on how to make the gelatine by boiling up calves' feet. Thankfully we can now buy perfectly good gelatine (from animal sources or vegetarian) in pristine transparent sheets.

150ml **sweet white wine** (e.g. Muscat or Baumes de Venise)
50g **caster sugar**
1 stick of **cinnamon**
450ml **fresh blood orange juice** (5 or 6 oranges)
4 leaves of **gelatine** (about 40g)

1. Put the wine into a pan with the sugar, the cinnamon stick and 150ml of the orange juice. Bring to the boil, then take off the heat and remove the cinnamon. Melt the gelatine into the juice (following the instructions on the packet).

2. Pour the rest of the orange juice into a jug and pour in the liquid from the pan. Stir thoroughly, then pour into your mould. Allow to cool, then put into the fridge until set.

3. To turn out, loosen the edges of the jelly gently with your fingers. Dip the mould into a bowl of hot water for 1–2 seconds, place a plate on top, then invert the mould and shake. Serve with single cream or light double cream.

TIPS

* Richard Olney uses orange and lemon juice rather than blood orange juice. You can experiment with all sorts of liquids: white wines, elderflower cordial, pomegranate, grapefruit and lime juice are all good.

* Try flavouring the jelly with herbs and spices – rosemary with orange, for example, or cardamom with coconut milk.

* We prefer a lighter set. Use less gelatine where you can get away with it.

* Try putting whole fruit inside your jelly (grapes, peach slices, strawberries, currants, etc). You can make the fruit float if you set a layer of jelly first, then add the fruit followed by the rest of the jelly.

* Some fruits have enzymes that digest jelly, which will make it hard to set. These include: figs, kiwis, mango, melon, papaya, peach, pineapple and ginger.

WINTER WARMERS

Hot Chocolate 5 Ways

SERVES 1 • PREPARATION TIME: 2 MINUTES • COOKING TIME: 10 MINUTES • V

Warming and reassuring, it's a hug in a mug. Here are our top five:

The Building Block Choc

The basic hot chocolate from which all the others (in this book) descend.

> 1 mug of **milk**
> 25–30g **good-quality dark chocolate**, grated

1. Heat the milk gently in a small saucepan. As soon as it reaches scalding point but before it boils, whisk in the grated chocolate until it has all melted thoroughly into the milk. (This has the added bonus of frothing everything up a bit.)

2. Pour out into your mug and serve.

Mexican Hot Chocolate

Add a stick of cinnamon, a good grating of orange zest and a pinch of chilli powder to give your chocolate a South of the Border feel. Arriba!

Swedish Hot Chocolate

Adults Only … well, you know what we mean … add a good slug of vodka and pop an Abba track on the stereo.

Natasha & Eleanor's Hot Chocolate

Top the Building Block Choc with a good sprinkling of mini marshmallows and plenty of whipped cream.

Jamaican Hot Chocolate

Stir it up with a good pinch of freshly ground allspice and a slug of Jamaican rum. Now we be chillin'.

TIPS

* We're using a good dark chocolate here so we can avoid all the added sugar, etc. you'll find in powdered drinking chocolate.

* All recipes these days bang on about 'good-quality chocolate'. They'll then go on to specify a minimum of cocoa solids in the chocolate, and so on. In this case, the flavour of the dark chocolate absolutely determines the flavour of your hot chocolate, so buy the brand you like. We love Original Beans – for their flavour, of course, but also for their fantastic work in the conservation of threatened rainforests and sustainable farming practices.

Hot Hallowe'en Punch

It was a Hallowe'en party in 2009, and Giles had the idea of making a hot punch – it was freezing outside. We used various bits and bobs that he found in the kitchen and came up with this. The party went with a swing, and this concoction is now a must every Hallowe'en.

400ml **brandy**
1.5 litres **West Country dry cider**
10 tablespoons **sugar**
300ml **lemon juice**
10 dashes of **Angostura bitters**
2–3 **cinnamon sticks**
5–6 **cloves**
lemon zest, to garnish

1. Pour all the ingredients except the lemon zest into a large pan and bring to a slow simmer.

2. Ladle into beakers and garnish with a twist of lemon zest.

Christmas Cocktail

SERVES 1 • PREPARATION TIME: 2 MINUTES • COOKING TIME: NONE • GF DF V

Tom made this last Christmas for his family. His mum loved it, and his dad drank far too much of it. Substitute berry cordial for Campari and use soda water instead of prosecco, then the kids can join in, too.

120ml **Campari**
60ml **lemon juice**
120ml **clementine juice**
70ml **Simple Syrup** (see recipe page 32)
420ml **prosecco**
orange zest, to garnish

1. In a cocktail shaker combine the Campari, lemon juice, clementine juice and sugar syrup.

2. Add ice and shake.

3. Strain the mixture equally into 6 champagne glasses and top with prosecco. Garnish with a twist of orange zest.

Glogg

SERVES 10–12 • STEEPING TIME: 2–4 HOURS • HEATING TIME: 20 MINUTES • V

Kay got this recipe from her mum and dad, who in turn got it from Scandinavian friends in Bangkok back in the day … It will certainly make a Christmas party go with a swing!

1 bottle of **vodka**
1 bottle of **red wine**
5 **cardamom pods,** cracked open
5 **cloves**
1 **stick of cinnamon**
1 piece of **orange rind**
1 piece of **fresh ginger**
200–300g **sugar** (or to taste)
peeled **almonds** and **raisins** – a big handful of each, to serve

1. Mix all the ingredients and leave for 2–4 hours.

2. Heat the Glögg slowly. Do not boil.

3. Add the almonds and raisins just before serving.

Irish Coffee

SERVES 4 • PREPARATION TIME: 15 MINUTES • COOKING TIME: NONE • WF GF V

Smooth and creamy, a proper Irish coffee is deeply warming and sinfully delicious.

> freshly brewed **hot coffee** (enough for 4)
> 4 teaspoons **brown sugar**
> 8 tablespoons **Irish whiskey**
> 225ml **double cream**, very lightly whipped
> 4 **Irish coffee glass mugs**

1. Make a fresh pot of coffee.

2. Place a teaspoon of brown sugar in the bottom of each Irish coffee mug and then pour in the hot coffee, leaving about 2–3cm room at the top of the mug. Stir gently.

3. Add 2 tablespoons of Irish whiskey to each mug.

4. Pour the barely whipped cream over the back of a spoon and into the mug.

TIPS

* The sugar and alcohol both help to float the cream on top, creating the look of a pint of Guinness, so do not omit them.

* The idea is that you sip the Irish coffee slowly through the cream, so it is important that the cream is not too stiff.

Vodka Espresso

SERVES 1 • PREPARATION TIME: 1 MINUTE • COOKING TIME: NONE • V

This drink has been a favourite of the London bar scene since the mid-nineties. Rumour has it that its birthplace was the Pharmacy – Damien Hirst's now defunct joint in Notting Hill. An experienced barman can tell how many of these caffeine-loaded cocktails a customer has had from the twitching in the arm or the judder of the head. Be warned: after three it is almost impossible to sit down.

40ml **vodka**
20ml **Kahlua**
35ml **espresso**
caster sugar
coffee beans to garnish (optional)

1. In a cocktail shaker combine the vodka, Kahlua, espresso and a dash of sugar (it's up to you how sweet you like it). Pack it full of ice and shake it really hard for about 10 seconds: you want a nice froth on top, so shake it good.

2. Pour into a martini glass or champagne flute and garnish with 3 coffee beans if you have them.

3. This recipe is for one cocktail. You can probably fit two in one shaker, but any more than that and you'll lose the lovely crème on top.

CONVERSION CHART FOR COMMON MEASURE

LIQUIDS

15 ml	1/2 fl oz
25 ml	1 fl oz
50 ml	2 fl oz
75 ml	3 fl oz
100ml	3 1/2 fl oz
125 ml	4 fl oz
150 ml	1/4 pint
175 ml	6 fl oz
200 ml	7 fl oz
250 ml	8 fl oz
275 ml	9 fl oz
300 ml	1/2 pint
325 ml	11 fl oz
350 ml	12 fl oz
375 ml	13 fl oz
400 ml	14 fl oz
450 ml	3/4 pint
475 ml	16 fl oz
500 ml	17 fl oz
575 ml	18 fl oz
600 ml	1 pint
750 ml	1 1/4 pints
900 ml	1 1/2 pints
1 litre	1 3/4 pints
1.2 litres	2 pints
1.5 litres	2 1/2 pints
1.8 litres	3 pints
2 litres	3 1/2 pints
2.5 litres	4 pints
3.6 litres	6 pints

WEIGHTS

5 g	1/4 oz
15 g	1/2 oz
20 g	3/4 oz
25 g	1 oz
50 g	2 oz
75 g	3 oz
125 g	4 oz
150 g	5 oz
175 g	6 oz
200 g	7 oz
250 g	8 oz
275 g	9 oz
300 g	10 oz
325 g	11 oz
375 g	12 oz
400 g	13 oz
425 g	14 oz
475 g	15 oz
500 g	1 lb
625 g	1 1/4 lb
750 g	1 1/2 lb
875 g	1 3/4 lb
1 kg	2 lb
1.25 kg	2 1/2 lb
1.5 kg	3 lb
1.75 kg	3 1/2 lb
2 kg	4 lb

MEASUREMENTS

5 mm	$^1/_4$ inch
1 cm	$^1/_2$ inch
1.5 cm	$^3/_4$ inch
2.5 cm	1 inch
5 cm	2 inches
7 cm	3 inches
10 cm	4 inches
12 cm	5 inches
15 cm	6 inches
18 cm	7 inches
20 cm	8 inches
23 cm	9 inches
25 cm	10 inches
28 cm	11 inches
30 cm	12 inches
33 cm	13 inches

Key to Symbols/Nutritional Info

♥   LOW SATURATED FATS

✓   LOW GLYCEMIC (GI) LOAD

WF   WHEAT FREE

GF   GLUTEN FREE

DF   DAIRY FREE

V   VEGETARIAN

TIPS   COOKING TIPS, EXTRA INFORMATION AND ALTERNATIVE IDEAS

Index

First published in Great Britain in 2013 by Conran Octopus Limited,
a part of Octopus Publishing Group,
Endeavour House, 189 Shaftesbury Avenue, London WC2H 8JY
www.octopusbooks.co.uk

An Hachette UK Company
www.hachette.co.uk

This book includes a selection of previously published recipes taken from the following titles:
Leon Naturally Fast Food; Leon Baking & Puddings; Leon Family & Friends.

British Library Cataloguing-in-Publication Data.
A catalogue record for this book is available from the British Library.

Publisher: Alison Starling
Senior Editor: Sybella Stephens
Assistant Editor: Stephanie Milner
Art Director: Jonathan Christie
Art Direction, Design and Illustrations: Anita Mangan
Design Assistant: Abigail Read
Photography: Georgia Glynn Smith
Production Manager: Katherine Hockley

ISBN 978 1 84091 621 8

Printed in China

A note from the authors…
We have endeavoured to be as accurate as possible in all the preparation and cooking times
listing in the recipes in this book. However they are an estimate based on our own timings
during recipe testing, and should be taken as a guide only, not as the literal truth. We have
also tried to source all our food facts carefully, but we are not scientists. So our food facts and
nutrition advice are not absolute. If you feel you require consultation with a nutritionist, consult
your GP for a recommendation.